RECEIVED

JUL 1 4 2009
GREENWOOD LIBRARY

NO LONGER PROPERTY
SEATTLE PUBLIC LIBRARY

WE THE PEOPLE

English Colonies in America

by Rebecca Love Fishkin

Content Adviser: Richard J. Bell, Ph.D.,
Assistant Professor, Department of History,
University of Maryland

Reading Adviser: Alexa L. Sandmann, Ed.D.,
Professor of Literacy, College and Graduate School of Education,
Kent State University

Compass Point Books ✦ Minneapolis, Minnesota

Compass Point Books
151 Good Counsel Drive
P.O. Box 669
Mankato, MN 56002-0669

Copyright © 2009 by Compass Point Books
All rights reserved. No part of this book may be reproduced without written permission from the
publisher. The publisher takes no responsibility for the use of any of the materials or methods
described in this book, nor for the products thereof.
Printed in the United States of America.

 This book was manufactured with paper containing
at least 10 percent post-consumer waste.

On the cover: The settlement of Jamestown, Virginia, in 1607: 19th century colored engraving

Photographs ©: The Granger Collection, New York, cover, 4, 7, 17, 24, 31, 32, 36, 38, 39; Prints
Old and Rare, back cover (far left); Library of Congress, back cover, 15, 22, 25; Drawing by A.S.
Warren for Ballou's Pictorial Drawing-Room Companion, April 7, 1855, from Charles de Volpi,
Newfoundland: a Pictorial Record (Sherbrooke, Quebec: Longman Canada Limited), 6; Burstein
Collection/Corbis, 9, 21; North Wind Picture Archives, 11, 12, 13, 16, 19, 28, 29, 34, 35; Colonial
National Historical Park/National Parks Service, 27; Line of Battle Enterprise, 41.

Editor: Jennifer VanVoorst
Page Production: Bobbie Nuytten
Photo Researcher: Svetlana Zhurkin
Cartographer: XNR Productions, Inc.
Library Consultant: Kathleen Baxter

Art Director: LuAnn Ascheman-Adams
Creative Director: Keith Griffin
Editorial Director: Nick Healy
Managing Editor: Catherine Neitge

Library of Congress Cataloging-in-Publication Data
Fishkin, Rebecca, 1972–
  English colonies in America / by Rebecca Fishkin.
    p. cm. — (We the people)
  Includes index.
  ISBN 978-0-7565-3838-5 (library binding)
  1. United States—History—Colonial period, ca. 1600–1775—Juvenile literature. I. Title. II. Series.
  E188.F5295 2009
  973.2—dc22   2008007210

Visit Compass Point Books on the Internet at *www.compasspointbooks.com*
or e-mail your request to *custserv@compasspointbooks.com*

TABLE OF CONTENTS

A New World

On September 5, 1774, a group of men gathered in Philadelphia to discuss freedom. They were representatives of the British colonies in North America, and the meeting was called the First Continental Congress. For a long time, the colonists had been taxed and bullied by Britain. They were ready for change, but each colony had different

The First Continental Congress opened with a prayer on September 5, 1774.

4

interests. The men spent many days arguing about what they wanted.

Then Patrick Henry, a representative from Virginia, made a passionate speech. He said it was time for the colonies to put aside their differences for a common cause. "The distinctions between Virginians, Pennsylvanians, New Yorkers and New Englanders are no more," he said. "I am not a Virginian, but an American."

It was an important statement that reflected the way that colonists were starting to feel. The men began to talk about common goals for America, not as 13 separate colonies, but as one united group seeking rights from Britain. It had taken more than 250 years to get that far.

The story of England's presence in the New World begins in 1497. That year, John Cabot explored North America in the name of England. He was searching for a northwest passage, a sea route through the continent that would allow European traders easier access to the spice markets of Asia. He did not find what he was looking

John Cabot planted an English flag on North American soil.

for, but as a result of his travels, England laid claim to the
continent of North America. But this claim was in name
only. It wasn't until the late 1500s that England made any
attempt to settle the New World.

In 1584, Queen Elizabeth I gave nobleman Sir Walter
Raleigh a charter to explore and colonize North America.
Raleigh made two attempts to establish colonies on Roanoke
Island, off the coast of North Carolina. Both failed. After

a difficult year, the first group of colonists gave up and returned to England. The second group, made up of more than 100 settlers, disappeared without a trace. The fate of this "lost colony" is still unknown.

In 1607, England finally established itself on the continent with a permanent settlement in Jamestown, Virginia. Life was difficult in Jamestown, but the settlers

Jamestown colonists created a new life for themselves in North America.

persevered. Native Americans taught them how to hunt, fish, and farm. New settlers arrived in 1608 and 1609, expanding the colony.

With the success of Jamestown, England quickly increased the pace of colonization. It soon became one of the most important countries to settle North America. England was competing with its rivals, Spain and France, for settlements. Spain had a presence in Florida and in the Southwest, and France had fur-trading posts along northern rivers and in Canada. England wanted to establish permanent colonies for long-term wealth, as well as a place to send people who disagreed with the king's religion and politics.

English citizens seeking religious freedom, land ownership, and adventure sailed across the Atlantic Ocean. It was a dangerous journey, and the colonists had to bring many supplies, including clothing, seeds, building materials, tools, weapons, and livestock. The settlers had to build homes, clear farmland, create governments, and learn how

English colonists braved rough seas on the way to the New World.

to survive in a strange land.

The English colonies were clustered along the Atlantic coast for easy trade with England and because inland mountains and forests were difficult to explore. Soon geography and religion shaped three distinct regions: New England, the Middle Atlantic, and the South. Cold, rocky New England was not good for farming and became a

England's 13 American colonies can be grouped into three distinct regions.

trade-centered society with strong religious leadership. The Middle Atlantic, with good soil and large cities, became known for religious tolerance. The warm, fertile South was ideal for farming.

SELF-GOVERNMENT

There were three types of English colonies in America. The first type was a proprietary colony, one given by the king to an individual or company. The second type was a chartered colony, one granted to a group of settlers. The third type was a royal colony, which was the property of the king. Many settlements that began as proprietary later became royal colonies. But with the king of England so far away, the colonists were left to govern themselves. Each colony had a governor, a council, and a body of elected representatives called an assembly. This was similar to the English government,

Colonial government was modeled after the English Parliament.

with its king and two houses of Parliament.

The governor was appointed by the king or proprietors to oversee all colony activities, including building the militia and granting land to settlers. The members of the council also were appointed. They were wealthy, well-respected colonists who advised the governor and made legislative and judicial decisions. Members of the assembly were elected by the colonists. Although it was the lower branch of government, the assembly was powerful because it set taxes and

The FRAME of the
GOVERNMENT
OF THE
𝕻𝖗𝖔𝖛𝖎𝖓𝖈𝖊 of 𝕻𝖊𝖓𝖓𝖘𝖎𝖑𝖛𝖆𝖓𝖎𝖆
IN
AMERICA
Together with certain
L A W S
Agreed upon in England
BY THE
GOVERNOUR
AND
Divers F R EE - M EN of the aforefaid
PROVINCE.

To be further Explained and Confirmed there by the firſt *Provincial Council* and *General Aſſembly* that ſhall be held, if they ſee meet.

Printed in the Year MDCLXXXII.

The title page of the document that outlined the laws of the colony of Pennsylvania

because it directly represented the colonists. When the assembly and the governor disagreed, the elected men often withheld money until their demands were met.

Local government differed by region. Each New England town elected its own men to make local laws. In the South, elected officials represented larger areas called counties or parishes. The Middle Atlantic colonies had both town and county governments. In all 13 colonies, only free men, not women or slaves, could vote or hold an elected position.

John Archdale, an early governor of Carolina, addressed the colonial assembly.

13

NEW ENGLAND: PURITANS, TOWNS, AND TRADE

The first New England colonists arrived aboard the *Mayflower* in 1620. Known as the Pilgrims, they came to the New World in search of religious freedom. Back home, the king required that all English citizens follow the Church of England. Those who had different beliefs were jailed and shunned. The Pilgrims wanted to worship as they wished in a land of their own. Other passengers on the *Mayflower* came in search of adventure and riches. The colonists were supposed to land in Virginia, but they ended up much farther north. They decided to stay, and they established Plymouth Colony, about 34 miles (54 kilometers) southeast of present-day Boston.

After docking in Cape Cod, the colonists wrote the Mayflower Compact, an agreement stating they would create and follow laws for the "general good of the colony." This led to the election of representatives who would speak

Colonists signed the Mayflower Compact, an agreement to set laws for their new home.

for the people. These elected officers were in charge of security, town supplies, and legal issues.

Not long after the Pilgrims settled at Plymouth Colony, a group called the Puritans also left England to practice their religion in America. They settled at Massachusetts Bay in 1630 and established the Massachusetts Bay Colony. In 1691, Plymouth joined

Boston and other nearby settlements to become part of the Massachusetts Bay Colony.

The Massachusetts Bay Colony was the first of the colonies in the region known as New England. With long, snowy winters and rocky hills, New England was not ideal for farming. But it was rich in many natural resources. There were thick forests and many rivers, and the ocean was full of fish, especially cod. The colonists built sawmills

Boston was the most important city in colonial New England.

and boats, becoming loggers, shipbuilders, fishermen, and merchants. New Englanders exported raw materials, including salted fish, to the Caribbean in exchange for other items, such as molasses and sugar. The colonists turned the molasses and sugar into rum, which was sent to England in exchange for other items, such as guns and cloth. These English goods were then taken to Africa, where they were traded for enslaved men, women, and children. The

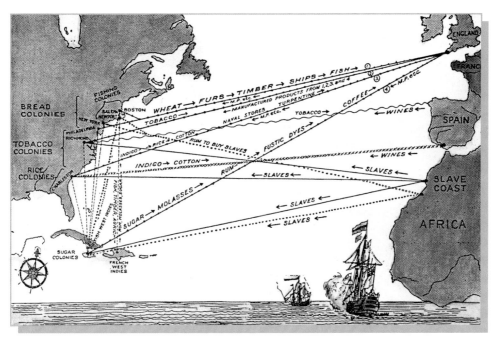

A 17th-century map depicts trade among Europe, North America, and Africa.

17

Africans were brought to the Caribbean to be sold as slaves. This became known as the Triangle Trade, and the city of Boston became a thriving port.

Most people in Massachusetts worked and lived in small towns. Townspeople held regular meetings to discuss government, schools, business, and community issues. However, the most important aspect of town life was religion. Puritans strictly followed the Bible and believed that good works would earn God's favor. They believed God sent sickness, Indian raids, and other disasters as punishment, so the colonists were expected to attend church and live strictly.

Although the Puritans had traveled to Massachusetts for religious freedom, they did not tolerate others with different beliefs. People who disagreed were punished or banished. Some established new colonies.

Roger Williams was a preacher who came to Massachusetts because his ideas of freedom of worship were criticized in England. In New England, his opinions about

Puritans gathered to worship according to their strict religious beliefs.

the separation of church and state angered the Puritans, and he was banished. Williams headed south, where he started a settlement called Providence in 1636. A year later, another Massachusetts resident, Anne Hutchinson, was banished for holding Bible study meetings and openly questioning Puritan beliefs. She helped start a settlement near Providence, called Portsmouth. The two settlements

19

became part of the Rhode Island Colony. Rhode Island was unique because its laws said residents had complete religious freedom, making it safe for Quakers, Jews, and others who disagreed with the Puritans.

Other colonists began to look beyond Massachusetts. Many started farms in the more fertile land around the Connecticut River, or they went north for land and fur trading. Anne Hutchinson's brother-in-law, John Wheelwright, was banished from Boston for supporting her. He started a settlement in what would become New Hampshire. The settlers created an agreement similar to the Mayflower Compact for governance.

Another clergyman, Thomas Hooker, fled Massachusetts to the Dutch settlement of Hartford. He declared that the settlement would have religious freedom and, in 1639, wrote the Fundamental Orders, which outlined a people-led government. In 1662, the settlement became the colony of Connecticut. Rhode Island and Connecticut were the first colonies to elect all of their own

Hooker's Party Coming to Hartford *was painted in 1846 by Frederic Edwin Church.*

officials, including the governor, and they had the most political independence from England.

Rhode Island, Connecticut, and New Hampshire modeled their town governments after Massachusetts, with elected men holding regular meetings. In similar ways, but for different reasons, all four New England colonies were working to build the New World into a permanent home away from England.

21

THE MIDDLE ATLANTIC: BIG CITIES AND RELIGIOUS TOLERANCE

In 1681, England's King Charles II gave land to William Penn to start a refuge for the Society of Friends, or Quakers. The Quakers believed they could find God through silent reflection rather than church sermons and strict Bible

Quaker William Penn received land rights from England's King Charles II.

interpretation. They opposed war and viewed men and women as equals. Quakers were persecuted in England and Massachusetts. Penn looked at his land in North America as a "holy experiment," a place where Quakers could live and worship freely. The land was named Pennsylvania, meaning Penn's Woods, after Penn's father.

With gently sloping land, rich soil, and milder winters than New England, Pennsylvania was a successful farming colony. The colonists planted a variety of crops, including many grains, and raised livestock such as cattle and sheep.

As governor, Penn insisted on low taxes and designed a government where men could feel represented and free. He traded peacefully with the Lenape Indians and began to build Philadelphia, known as the City of Brotherly Love, on the banks of the Delaware River. Penn had noted how crowded conditions in London contributed to fire and disease, so he designed Philadelphia differently. He plotted grids of streets, with parks and land surrounding homes for open, green space.

23

Philadelphia was true to Penn's vision of religious tolerance and diversity, with Germans, Scotch-Irish, Swedish, and Dutch settlers from surrounding farmland joining English residents. By the 18th century, it had become the largest city in North America and was a cultural center.

North of Pennsylvania, the Dutch colony of New Netherland had fertile river valleys for livestock and crops,

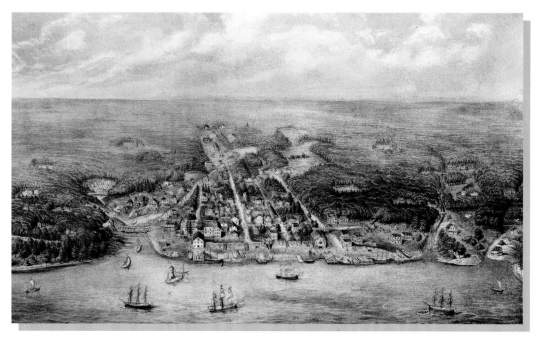

Philadelphia harbor in the early 1700s

such as apples and flax. The Hudson River was a major route for fur traders, but the early English colonists stayed mostly east of the river. The Dutch paid the Indians in goods worth $24 for a small island known as Manhattan. It soon became the bustling trade center of New Amsterdam, which was known for diversity and tolerance. Before Philadelphia boomed, the city was the largest in the Middle Atlantic.

In 1664, England took New Amsterdam without firing a single shot. The English renamed the colony New York. Eventually, it formed an elected assembly like other colonies, and local government was divided into counties.

Delaware and New Jersey also were

Dutch soldiers peacefully left New Amsterdam after the English captured the city.

first settled by the Dutch. Delaware changed hands from Dutch to Swedish and back, until 1674, when England took the land. The king gave Delaware to William Penn, but it later became a separate colony. New Jersey was pieced together from parts of New York and Pennsylvania. Settled by Puritans to the east and Quakers to the west, New Jersey became a separate colony in 1702.

New Jersey and Delaware had good soil, flat land, and a moderate climate, so farming became the main lifestyle. There were no big cities, only small towns that modeled their governments after New England's. Both colonies mostly echoed the religious tolerance of Pennsylvania.

The Middle Atlantic bridged the gap between New England's small towns and the South's sprawling plantations. Philadelphia and New York offered intellectual and cultural development unlike the other regions. But perhaps the strongest difference was the overall religious tolerance offered by the four Middle Atlantic colonies.

THE SOUTH: FIRST COLONY AND TOBACCO PLANTATIONS

The South was the site of the first permanent English settlement, Jamestown, in the colony of Virginia. Led by Captain John Smith, about 100 colonists arrived in 1607 and settled on the banks of the James River. Virginia had good farmland, many rivers, and a warm climate. Still, Indian attacks, disease, poor crops, and starvation almost led the colonists to abandon the settlement.

Jamestown was named after King James I of England.

Then a colonist named John Rolfe began to grow tobacco. The colonists did not like the native tobacco grown by Indians, preferring sweeter leaves grown by the Spanish in the Caribbean and imported by England. Rolfe planted Caribbean seeds in Virginia and tended them until he had a successful crop. It became Virginia's first profitable export.

Tobacco plantations became the center of Southern life, which was much more rural than the Middle Atlantic and New England. Except for the port cities, there were

Colonists tended the tobacco crop in colonial Virginia.

few towns, and the large plantations were far apart in fertile river valleys.

Unlike the Middle Atlantic and New England, the majority of the colonists who settled in the South were seeking land and wealth, rather than religious freedom. Plantation owners held political power. They owned the land and employed many colonists. They also owned slaves.

Slavery was introduced to the colonies in 1619, when a Dutch ship arrived in Jamestown bearing 20 kidnapped Africans. The trader sold the Africans to plantation owners, who put them to work as unpaid laborers.

Slavery existed in North America for nearly 250 years.

29

These enslaved people—and the generations who followed—endured terrible conditions on their voyage across the Atlantic. They fared no better once they arrived in America. As human property, they had no freedom, and they were punished harshly if they resisted their fate.

The practice of slavery separated the South from the other regions. Some colonists in New England and the Middle Atlantic owned slaves, but slavery was much more widespread in the South. The enslaved people on Southern plantations also lived under much harsher conditions with less hope of freedom. Long after the Revolutionary War, slavery continued to cause a major divide between North and South.

The year 1619 was historic in Virginia for another reason. That year, the first representative meeting in North America was held in Jamestown. Its goal was to establish a government for the colony. The elected body was called the House of Burgesses, and it made the laws for Virginia. It became the model for other colonies' elected assemblies and

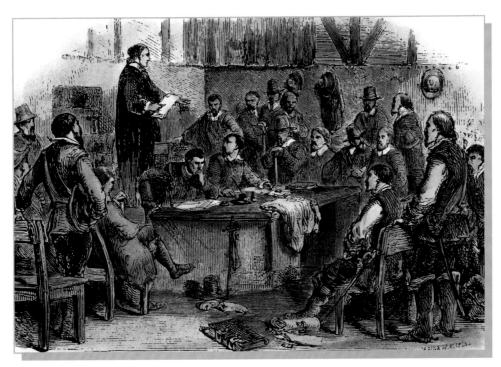

A 19th-century engraving of the 1619 meeting of the House of Burgesses

demonstrated how much the colonists valued having a say in government.

Bordering Virginia to the east was an enormous bay that would be named Chesapeake Bay. Many rivers fed into the bay, which met the Atlantic Ocean at its southern end, not far from Jamestown. This land became home to the one Southern colony specifically founded to provide religious freedom.

Sir George Calvert, the first Lord Baltimore, wanted land near the bay. He died before receiving land from King Charles I, but his son, Cecil, inherited the land grant and started the colony of Maryland. Settled in 1634, Maryland became as well-known as Philadelphia for religious tolerance and had a government similar to Virginia's. Baltimore, the colony's largest city, was built at the top of Chesapeake Bay as a port for tobacco trade.

Farther south, the colony of Carolina was chartered in 1663 and later split into North Carolina and South Carolina. With a climate similar to Virginia's,

The first Roman Catholic Mass in the colonies was performed in Maryland on March 25, 1634.

North Carolina produced tobacco, tar, and lumber. It had no major port because the coast was dangerous for ships, with small barrier islands and rocky coves.

South Carolina was warmer and more humid, with coastal palm trees and inland pine forests. In addition to lumber and tobacco, the colonists harvested rice grown in marshy lowlands. They also grew indigo, which made a deep blue dye valued in England. The port of Charles Town, which was later renamed Charleston, was a social and commercial hub.

The last British colony in North America had a different start. James Oglethorpe was a member of the British government who wanted to help people who had been jailed for debt. He proposed a colony that would be a refuge for prisoners. The king liked the idea of getting rid of debtors. England also needed to protect its land from the Spanish, who had settlements in Florida. In 1732, King George II granted a 21-year charter for land south of the Carolinas. Oglethorpe was appointed

James Oglethorpe and his colonists were greeted by Native Americans.

governor of this colony, called Georgia, and started a
settlement called Savannah.

Georgia produced rice, indigo, and lumber. It was
the only colony that received money through a vote in
the British Parliament. It also had a board of trustees that
made the laws for the colony. While colonists could have
free land for 10 years, they had no say in government. This
changed in 1752, when Georgia became a royal colony.

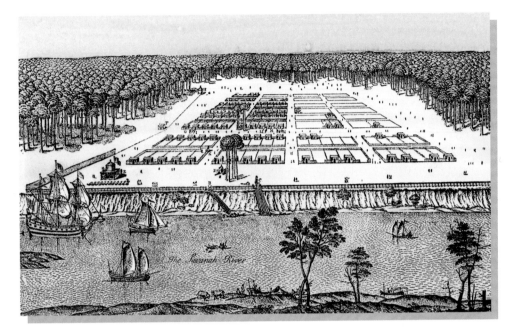

Savannah, Georgia, in 1741

Then the colonists adopted a self-governing system more like the other colonies. They also stopped importing English prisoners and started importing African slaves.

Their rural lifestyle set them apart from New England and the Middle Atlantic, but the Southern colonists shared the same desire as their northern neighbors. They wanted the freedom to make their own laws and wealth in North America.

UNITING FOR INDEPENDENCE

By the middle of the 1700s, better transportation had improved communication between the colonies. Boats sailed up and down the coast, and by 1711, a road connected New York and Boston. By 1732, stagecoaches were carrying goods and passengers, who no longer had to walk on old Indian trails. The colonies were beginning to feel more

By the 18th century, colonists traveled by stagecoach.

connected, and they found that they shared a growing anger toward Britain.

Britain was often at war with France and Spain, both abroad and in North America. The colonies were often left alone, and the colonists liked the sense of independence. But Britain recognized the importance of the colonies' trade, and it created restrictions to keep the wealth. Britain passed the Navigation Acts, which said trade of valuable goods to and from the colonies could be done only on British ships with British crews. All goods had to go through Britain, including tobacco, sugar, rice, furs, hats, molasses, and iron.

Beginning in 1754, Britain fought the French over control of the colonies. The conflict, known as the French and Indian War, ended in 1763 with a British victory. As a result, the British took control of all French territory in North America. After the war, King George III looked to the colonies to raise money to pay Britain's war debts.

In 1765, the British Parliament passed the Stamp Act, taxing all printed paper used by the colonists, including

Colonists in Boston read about the Stamp Act in August 1765.

newspapers and legal documents. Playing cards and dice also were taxed. The colonists were angry that Britain had set a tax without discussing it with their own legislatures. They boycotted British products and did not use the stamps. Britain repealed the tax.

In 1773, Britain passed the Tea Act, forcing colonists to buy tea only from the British East India Company. The colonists refused to unload British tea from ships and barred the ships from entering ports. On December 16, 1773, a group of colonists called the Sons of Liberty boarded three

British ships in Boston Harbor and dumped all of the tea overboard. The event was known as the Boston Tea Party.

Britain responded by passing more restrictions, which the colonists called the Intolerable Acts. Britain closed the port of Boston, limited self-government in Massachusetts,

An 1845 engraving of the Boston Tea Party

and required colonists to allow British troops to stay in their homes.

The colonists decided it was time to stand up to Britain. In 1774, the First Continental Congress convened in Philadelphia. Only Georgia did not send representatives, because it wanted to keep British soldiers to help defend its borders against the Spanish. The colonists drafted a list of complaints and demands for King George III and agreed to meet again if their needs were not met.

The colonies began to consider taking military action against the British. At the Virginia House of Burgesses, Patrick Henry again made a speech that moved colonial leaders to action. He said, "Is life so dear, or peace so sweet, as to be purchased at the price of chains and slavery? Forbid it, Almighty God! I know not what course others may take, but as for me, give me liberty or give me death!"

On April 19, 1775, British troops and colonial militia fired shots at each other at Lexington and Concord in Massachusetts. In May, the Second Continental Congress

Patrick Henry gave his famous speech to the House of Burgesses in 1775.

convened. The colonists were ready to fight for freedom, and they chose George Washington to lead their army.

On July 4, 1776, the 13 colonies unanimously passed the Declaration of Independence, stating that they were no longer part of Britain. The colonies, now the United States of America, had united for revolution.

GLOSSARY

charter—official document granting permission to set up a new colony, organization, or company

colony—territory settled by people from another country and controlled by that country

debtors—people who owe money to other people or companies

export—goods produced in one location and sold to another

House of Burgesses—representative assembly of colonial Virginia

plantations—large farms in the South, usually worked by slaves

proprietary—ownership or exclusive rights to something held by an individual or a group

self-government—government of a location or organization by its own people

tolerance—acceptance of people's beliefs or actions that differ from one's own beliefs or actions

unanimously—agreed upon by all parties

DID YOU KNOW?

- Members of the Society of Friends were called Quakers because they were said to "tremble at the name of the Lord."

- King George II wanted the colonists to produce silk in Georgia. He ordered them to plant mulberry trees, which feed silkworms, but the trees did not survive in the Southern climate, and the plan was abandoned.

- To avoid paying taxes or buying only British goods, the colonists often cooperated with pirates. The pirate Blackbeard, who was a British citizen named Edward Teach, had a home base in North Carolina. The colony's leaders made a deal with him to buy goods, such as cloth and sugar. The governor of Virginia decided to stop Blackbeard and sent attack ships to capture him. Blackbeard was killed in the fight.

- When Georgia was founded in 1733, it was the only British colony that did not allow slavery. However, before long, the need for plantation labor made slavery a reality in Georgia, too. In 1750, it was the last of the 13 colonies to legalize slavery.

IMPORTANT DATES

Timeline

1607	Colonists establish a settlement in Jamestown, Virginia.
1619	The slave trade begins in the colonies; Jamestown colonists hold the first meeting of the House of Burgesses.
1620	Pilgrims arrive in Massachusetts aboard the *Mayflower*.
1634	The Calverts settle Maryland.
1636	Roger Williams starts the Providence settlement in Rhode Island.
1639	Thomas Hooker writes the Fundamental Orders in Connecticut.
1664	England claims New Amsterdam from the Dutch, which becomes New York.
1681	William Penn receives a charter for Pennsylvania.
1732	James Oglethorpe receives a charter for Georgia.
1776	On July 4, the 13 colonies approve the Declaration of Independence.

IMPORTANT PEOPLE

GEORGE CALVERT (1580?–1632)

The first Lord Baltimore who requested land to start the colony of Maryland; he died before it was granted, so his son, Cecil (1605–1675), was given the land; he served King James I as secretary of state and was a member of the English Parliament

ANNE HUTCHINSON (1591–1643)

Massachusetts resident banished for her beliefs; she helped found Portsmouth, which later became part of Rhode Island; she moved to New York in 1642 after her husband died; she was murdered there by Indians the following year

WILLIAM PENN (1644–1718)

Quaker who founded Pennsylvania and the city of Philadelphia; in England, he was imprisoned several times for preaching about Quakerism; as governor of Pennsylvania, his treaties with Native Americans were so fair that they never attacked the colony

ROGER WILLIAMS (1603?–1683)

Preacher banished from Massachusetts who helped start the colony of Rhode Island as a religious refuge; Williams was a strong supporter of the separation of church and state and wrote a book about this belief; he also wrote a dictionary of Native American language

WANT TO KNOW MORE?

More Books to Read

Burgan, Michael. *Colonial America.* Chicago: Heinemann Library, 2006.

Connell, Kate. *The Thirteen Colonies.* Washington, D.C.: National
    Geographic Society, 2006.

Hakim, Joy. *Making Thirteen Colonies*: New York: Oxford University
    Press, 2005.

Micklos, John. *From Thirteen Colonies to One Nation.* Berkeley Heights, N.J.:
    Enslow Publishers, 2008.

On the Web

For more information on this topic, use FactHound.

1. Go to *www.facthound.com*

2. Type in this book ID: 0756538386

3. Click on the *Fetch It* button.

FactHound will find the best Web sites for you.

On the Road

Jamestown Settlement and Yorktown Victory Center

P.O. Box 1607

Williamsburg, VA 23187

757/253-4838 or 888/593-4682

Galleries and outdoor replicas of life in 17th-century Virginia

Historic Philadelphia

500 Arch St.

Philadelphia, PA 19106

215/629-5801

Independence Hall, the Liberty Bell, and other sites in the City of Brotherly Love

Look for more We the People books about this era:

African-Americans in the Colonies

The California Missions

Dutch Colonies in America

The French and Indian War

French Colonies in America

The Jamestown Colony

The Mayflower Compact

The Plymouth Colony

The Salem Witch Trials

Spanish Colonies in America

The Stamp Act of 1765

The Thirteen Colonies

Williamsburg

Women of Colonial America

A complete list of We the People titles is available on our Web site: www.compasspointbooks.com

INDEX

About the Author

Rebecca Love Fishkin has written for newspapers, magazines, and Web sites. This is her first book for young readers. She has managed an early literacy program and worked in the communications department of an international nonprofit organization that repairs children's cleft lips and palates. She lives in Lawrenceville, New Jersey.